All the World
at Once

BOOKS BY GREG WATSON

What Music Remains (2011)
The Distance Between Two Hands (2008)
Things You Will Never See Again (2006)
Pale Light from a Distant Room (2004)
Cold Water Memory (2001)
Annmarie Revisions (2000) (chapbook)
Open Door, Open Wall (1998) (chapbook)

All the World
at Once

New and Selected Poems

Greg Watson

NODIN PRESS

ACKNOWLEDGMENTS

"First Snow," *Devil Blossoms;* "Landlocked," *Orbis;* "Hands," *Whistling Shade/ Curmudgeon;* "Figure in the Rain" and "Summer's End," *Naugahyde Literary Journal;* "In an Imaginary Barn Alone," *South Ash Press/ Thin Coyote;* "Pastoral," *Spout;* "The Loft" and "Arizona," *Sulphur River Literary Review;* "Let This Night be the Wine," *Pegasus;* "Winter, 1989," *Thin Coyote;* "Wait Long Enough and a Pattern Emerges," *Saint Paul Almanac / Writers' Journal;* "Love Poem to a Blue Radio," *Mind Purge;* "Frank Sinatra Changing Limos," *Nerve Cowboy* and to *The Wind Blows, the Ice Breaks: Poems of Loss and Renewal by Minnesota Poets* (Nodin Press); "Shard," *What Light;* "On Translation," *Free Lunch;* "A Good Day," *Lucid Moon;* "Moment," *What Light;* "Now," *Writers' Journal* and *The Writer's Almanac;* "Morning Poem," *Freefall, At the Table anthology;* "Midway Motel," *What Light, Saint Paul Almanac;* "On the Death of a Giraffe at Como Zoo," *Ship of Fools;* "Tornado," *Saint Paul Almanac;* "Washing Her Hair," *Kippis!;* "I Know," *The Indented Pillow;* "The Leaving," *What Light;* "My Brother's Tattoo," *What Light / Nerve Cowboy;* "At the Sparkle Laundromat," *Saint Paul Almanac;* "Landscape," *Whistling Shade;* "Each Day the Sun Makes Us," *Lilliput Review;* "Procession," *Sulphur River Literary Review;* "In the Wings," *Saint Paul Almanac;* "Elegy for the Hungry Mind Bookstore," *Living Here: Poems about Neighborhoods.* Special thanks to Sandy Anderson, Susanne Maldonado, Norton Stillman, and Margaret Hasse.

Cover art: Bryan Iwamoto
Design and layout: John Toren

Library of Congress Cataloging-in-Publication Data

Watson, Greg, 1970–
  [Poems. Selections]
  All the world at once : new and selected poems / Greg Watson.
    pages ; cm
  ISBN 978-1-935666-74-5
  I. Title.
  PS3623.A8723A6 2015
  811'.6--dc23

                                                    2014045624

Nodin Press, LLC
5114 Cedar Lake Road
Minneapolis, MN

CONTENTS

THREE:
Poems from *The Distance Between Two Hands* (2008)
What Music Remains (2011)

FOUR:
New Poems

ONE

*I wanted to understand
so much all at once
but learned:
to understand everything,
begin with one breath.*

— Albert Huffstickler

FIRST SNOW

It has come early this year,
dragging its bony silence through the streets
like the billowing ghost of Christ,
clothes heavy and white upon the line.
On every corner old men bend
their backs to the earth and spit,
talk of blizzards from decades past.
Cars stall; dogs step tentatively
upon the shifting ground.
Loose change echoes in newspaper stands,
the knife-sharp jangle of turning keys.
Someone has sketched an alphabet in the snow,
and the name Sofia. Sofia.
One continuous word
for the wind to simply blow away.

LANDLOCKED

You would never know the ocean exists but for the
affirmations of others, a postcard from a place where time
is measured by the pull of tides. You would never know the
moon too is liquid, hydrologic, a drum fit to burst. You would
accept the wind as temporary and dry, like cigar smoke blown
through the nostrils. You would drive through desert after
desert, writing love poems in a worn, blue notebook, drinking
whiskey as if it were the eternal substitute for water.

HANDS

The hands, you tell me, the hands
are glass keys, the navigators of distance,
weather vanes of wind, rain and bitter heart,
the framework of knotted fists.
The hands say more than eyes, elbows
and sex organs combined.
You are right, of course.
But the hands linger too long for safety.
They grope, grab, grapple with memories
the mind cannot recall,
reach for whiskey, cigarettes,
for warmth between the flesh and pulse
of good womanly thighs
in the black breath before dawn,
the same hours that drove ancient men to madness
on ships, in empty rooms and stone cells.
Sever them, good woman,
they are too raw.
They are too much responsibility.

FIGURE IN THE RAIN

In quiet repose you hold the doorway
upright, smoking as if smoking
were an act of God,
breathless glow of downcast face
amid streams of cinder-black hair,
wind-strewn shadows stretched
the very length of desire,
impossible spark of blood and stone
struck from the match
that smolders at your feet.

Woman among women, beautiful damage,
painter of broken wings,
now could I stand
bloodstream to bloodstream
with you and never want
for water again.

SUMMER'S END

The cat's dish is covered with cobwebs;
the sky, more ancient than usual,
cracks at the corners like a lost painting
discovered in an attic
after the war, its edges beginning
to peel, beginning to curl
like the wired spring
of an all-encompassing scroll.
Today is no one's birthday
and it tells you so.
The terror of summer leaves
is the terror of waking
and finding blueberries instead of knuckles:
a new season has awakened
and left you asleep
in the steps of passing strangers.
You throw your hands up and wait,
not knowing who or what for.

IN AN IMAGINARY
BARN ALONE

A small girl, red as a freckle,
swallowing books like doorways,
catching cannonballs in her choking hair.

A single cross hangs unevenly,
its silence stretched for miles, bearing
the weight of a thousand mourners.

And the blood you saw on the TV news,
so beautiful you'd have sworn
she'd live forever.

PASTORAL

Then the postman arrived with the month
of November, everything
suddenly gray as snakestone.
The women covered their flesh, the leaves
shook hands with the devil.
A song on the radio withered like grapes on the vine.
Trees hunkered down like old men
lighting cigars in the rain.
Someone sent a telegram to the sun saying:
Don't bother.
In its absence we ceased speaking
with the warmth of breath.
Everything went still and silent as a book
shelved in a closet. Everything
balanced on a simple white envelope.

THE LOFT

The winters were the worst, outwardly bitter,
jealous, minimalist to a fault
as we waded through, thick and clinging,
speaking softly as hostages,
staying in bed for days on end.
We were not sick but in love,
a separate and higher calling of illness
(or so I imagined in the fervor
of youth). The landmarks of your body
I knew and knew again – memorizing
what I could, yet could never fully know.
If I dressed or read books or bothered with food,
I was a fool. I should have known all along
the dangers inherent, that the slightest
of movements could startle you awake.
Though it was, while it was, the best –
black veils and roses hung upon the walls
like crosses, there in that simple room,
cathedral-high ceilings and Bach's death mask
gazing eyelessly toward the door,
toward the sprawling, snowbound city,
silent and deaf in its death-like knowledge,
as if all I say now were somehow foreseeable.

ARIZONA

We drove all day with the sun at our backs,
hours passing by like a series of dreams,
past red clay madonnas and the feet of God,
on through the belly and the poverty
of Navajo land, missing the Grand Canyon
by the length of its echo.

At the trading post outside of Flagstaff
they sold wooden crucifixes
besides half-melted Hershey bars
and belt buckles made from hood ornaments.
I bought ghost beads and went shirtless,
crawled atop an enormous rock
and parted the clouds with my bare hands.
"Beginner's luck," you said.

We brought whiskey and beer into the rez
and watched the sun set like a
cosmological cocktail.
Later, we slept in your mother's adobe,
cats jumping in and out of the washing machine
as a light blue snow fell upon the mountains
and we slept the unsteady sleep
of strangers – not to each other
but to the rest of the world:
the exact cross-stitch where the
long-stretched skin of the desert ends,
pushed ever backward by the wind-bent buildings
and great rivers named for men,
asthmatic cities with gravestone sidewalks,
and the endless highways required
to somehow keep them from falling apart.

BETWEEN TIMES

At times our lives are in unison,
the rhythm of our speech right in time,
body to body, breath to breath.
Lying fallow in wanton love
I accept, I take it all in,
the purest antidote for caustic grief,
the hedonist's fervor that shakes
the black years to ash.
Yet on gray days there is distance,
there is silence between spaces no wider
than flesh. We bruise more easily,
wear our clothing like war flags,
our jewelry like armor;
the scar on my arm raised
like a stem beneath the skin,
the bruise upon your thigh
a glinting shard of moonlight
wrapped in rainbow wax.
Though faith returns, begging and joyful,
the slapdash way sunlight hits
a warehouse in Lowertown,
or the ocean, how it reaches its
furthest destination without struggle,
yielding only to itself, beginning again.
Fire for fire, measure for measure,
I would not change it; I would not
trade it. Not for silver, not
for gold, not for any world I know.

PHOTOGRAPH FOUND IN THE SLEEVE OF A 78

Duchin performs Gershwin, the radio dial of the hi-fi lit
like the skyline of a distant city. A stack of 78s is playing,
the thick discs dropping one by one; between the notes a
crackling sound like rain heard through whisper-thin walls.
A slender young woman stands beside a small window, her
black taffeta dress unzipped near the neck where a lover's
hand might rest. She wears medium heels, silk stockings,
small, bright globes of earrings. Perhaps she is waiting for
someone far away now, waiting for the stars to assemble
and map the way home. Look closely and you can see the
Brooklyn Bridge, a blur of fog-bound skyscrapers, as if they
were somehow walking away. In the narrow white border
below, in a script like small rolling waves, someone has
written, simply enough: "Lela, January 14, 1942."

RAIN IN NEW ORLEANS

All day it came down like bullets, so heavy
and so fast it seemed an imitation
of rain. Gray taxis stalled

in the narrow streets, buildings and people
suddenly far away, grainy as
ancient tintypes. The museums

swelled and the music slowed to a waltz.
Tourists rushed by in bright summer clothes,
one-page concert programs creased

and creased again like overstuffed match-
books, their dime-store umbrellas
collapsing like broken corsets.

Brass bands huddled together like criminals
under wind-frayed awnings, and tap boys
danced shirtless on every corner,

sinewy as copperheads, solid as railroad iron,
so frantic, so furious that neither
wind nor rain could touch them.

PROCESSION

The autumn leaves grow brittle, curled
and clinging in the chill-damp air; old men
in coal-colored suits shuffle and smoke, buttonholes
blooming the gold of forgotten suns.

The long procession of automobiles,
cold and lacquered as museum pieces, crawls
grudgingly along the blacktop,
small, nationless flags waving from each.

A woman the age and pallor of the sidewalk
watches, arms folded against the wind,
mouths a name in silence
waiting for the light to change.

WINTER POEM

In deep winter the bones of the highway
crack beneath its frozen weight.
Plain dirt roads fill with ghosts,
casting shadows thin as nails.
Night bleeds into day like water into stone;
beer cans glint in swollen banks
of snow, proud as soldiers in formation.
In the distance, bare-knuckled trees
stretch like fractures in the empty sky,
gated refineries crackle and
smoke to keep us alive.
Now is the time to drink whiskey,
read the classics,
let whiskers grow white.
Now the poets brood like professionals,
cursing the wind which cuts through flesh like razors.
But the poet knows next to nothing;
for months he pines and prays for spring
and is soon complaining
of the mud on his underused boots.

RAIN MUSIC

This night, too cold for crickets or for stars, rain so silent
the grass is unsure. A violin on the radio is weeping. It is
the music of stoic-minded stars turning toward reflection,
the window glass beginning to breathe. It is a thousand
magnetic spiders stretching silk into light and light into
sound. It is all sound and all sorrow in linear transition,
from empty box to broken bottle, this endless distillation
of unused tears.

Such alchemy cannot last. Soon it will all fall like furniture,
like men, this city of light buried beneath the endless
clamor of armor. I turn the volume down, turn back to the
poem I was writing before writing this. I prefer the sound
of a single soul. I prefer the weeping.

ALL NIGHT THE SAME MOTH

All night the same moth
fluttering against
the broken window screen.
I could go on and on,
chasing it back into the waiting
darkness, neither of us
learning a thing.

CALICO

It's four in the morning, the television
receding to a soft blue haze an hour ago;
the city yawning through its alleys
the stale-sour breath of seasons past.

Brittle leaves the color of ancient papyrus
crawl the uneven curbs
in search of severed branches
to somehow drink and green themselves again.

Everyone is fattening their blood now,
in fear of the hollowness of winter bones,
in fear of a great silence that leaves
even the crickets mute.

The cats come and go, quick with intent,
white bellies low to the ground,
shaking off entire lifetimes
like pearls of imaginary water...

The night is filled
with the flavor of our longing.

TWO

To see the world and say it true
means starting with loss.

– Gregory Orr

LET THIS NIGHT BE THE WINE

Let this night be the wine
in which the drunken moon swims
and the pools of your eyes
the ink with which I puncture my skin.

I will bring forth your name
like the smallest of bones.
I will climb the length of your corvus hair
on a ladder of broken starlight.

What does it matter
if my own name is forgotten?
What does it matter if my soul is lost
in the landscape of your brow?

Let us speak the same language
this terrible, joyous evening,
our shadows stretched the length before us,
swaying from side to side.

STUDY FOR THE WORLD'S BODY

from a painting by R.B. Kitaj

The dancer's face is chalk-white and flat,
the window behind her full of winter,
its weight and persistence
cut and removed from walls red as the guts of a pomegranate,
red as the valentine
we remember from childhood.

Her long, thin fingers, practiced and elegant,
rest upon his shoulder - this man,
his face hot with blood and motion, whose dark visage
has emerged, angular as a doorframe, from
the four corners of the room.

But the hand appears detached,
hovering
or emerging from the wall -
a ghost-hand, perhaps, belonging to neither,
but to a third who moves between them
and measures the distance their movements have made,
and how long the earth will be gone
before it returns
to find them here again.

WINTER, 1989

She never kisses like someone just waking,
this strange woman I have found,
her lips full on the mouth,
moist, warm, wanting, the cool touch of her hands
on my face like bookends,
as the wax-like face of Christ
glows ghostly from a wall of rusted brick;
we are alone as two people together can be,
her boots in a pile of sludge
on the hardwood floor, her calico sweater
crumpled at the foot of the bed,
her gossamer nightgown soaked in sweat,
filaments of candlelight on the swell of her hip,
lunar, warm as mink, this small imposing body
which has caused me so much trouble that
I no longer read but in Braille, and
have no idea how I got here through all this snow.

LOVE POEM
IN THREE SEPARATE ROOMS

Where I live, your name is
a household, its whispered syllables

like three separate rooms
from which my fractured voice sings:

a white tree outside each window
and the shadow on the page lifted in flight.

HAVING RESCUED EVERY LETTER YOU WROTE, I LET THE HOUSE BURN DOWN

The pale blue stone from Lake Superior
will remain in the window.

Red stumps of smoldering candles
know nothing of irony.

Black sunlight filters through door frames.
Black soot blossoms on the tongue like berries.

Walls once solid collapse like burning canvas,
and the telephone melts into tar.

Night will come again soon, cold stars retracting
from their light, a shuffling of crow's wings

through wet grass and desk drawers
warped into the framework

of strange new instruments, trees
grown long and expansive in thick brown shadow.

And you, my love, who survived your worst
and prettiest years in these pallid rooms,

are nowhere to be found. Words,
those smallest of birds caught in mid-sentence,

now lie silent on the lawn, punctuated
by an order of late September ants.

Should you return, you will find little here
of consequence – a simple stone,

bleak skeleton of a marriage bed, a structure
even the wind refuses to touch.

WAIT LONG ENOUGH
AND A PATTERN EMERGES

Today the river cannot decide
which course to take,
like a young woman rushing out
the door, then back again
to change her shoes.

THE HORSES

We lie calmly, talking without talking,
upon the time-worn rocks that guard Superior,
those great sand-colored bodies
glistening like palominos in the sun.
All ambition has fled. Even the breeze
has little to do now with movement.
When the time comes to leave, we follow
the path the horses have taken, go
where they go when the sun
goes down.

INTERIORS

1
All rooms are formless,
their interiors dependent only on
the shape of others.

2
These doors that open
onto walls ...

They are no more doors
than the walls
themselves.

3
If each stanza is indeed a room,
each word must therefore be a window
and each line a doorway opening
into more and more doors
ad infinitum.

A LEAF

I recognize this leaf from another season,
caught in the window screen
above my desk, curled slightly
at edges and stem,
dull, withered, delicate
as memory, neither clinging
nor allowing itself
to fall.

A leaf such as this is a star
not quite, a puppet for wind and sun
where wind and sun stand still,
a face quietly burning
the longing of centuries:
dead already,
yet still looking in.

TRAVELING BY NIGHT

In the city, as trees fade and lengthen
into shadow, I am unable to speak of or imagine
anything resembling wilderness.
Even the birds here dream city dreams,
barely startle at the screams of passing sirens.
I lay my body down upon the earth,
a stranger in a world of passing strangers,
thoughts traveling downward,
beneath the level of discernible language or intent.
If I continue in this way, a forest may
at last be revealed, or a leaf-print calling me
brother through the cold dark.

PALIMPSEST

Early afternoon. Blue shadows cross
the walls like thoughts unfettered, shape-shifters
refusing to declare themselves as
tree, bird, stone, or human.
Limbs and bodies entwine briefly,
a dance of shudders and sighs
converging with the expanding darkness.
Perhaps we too are shadow,
cast by something larger
just beginning to stir, the shoulder
of a mountain at dusk, or a hand moving
slowly, methodically across the page.

FRANK SINATRA CHANGING LIMOS
(circa 1991)

Lessons in impermanence are everywhere. Once, when I was young, I saw Frank Sinatra after a performance step into one limousine, hunker down, and enter another. It was so seamless, so practiced, that no one seemed to notice. This is how death must be, I think. Others will be saddened, searching for us, confused, pounding their hands on the window of an empty car. Meanwhile, we'll be drinking Chevis Regal, talking to the president long distance, slowly pulling out into the dark and boundless night.

ELEGY FOR THE HUNGRY MIND BOOKSTORE
(1970 – 2004)

Walking past the bookstore late at night,
closed today after thirty-four years, I notice how
the bookcases resemble coffins lined up along the wall,
taking whatever light the moon will give them,
giving back nothing but silence, the dark blonde solitude
that takes up where words leave off.
I think of every poet who has passed through,
the unhurried persistence of their voices
lingering like mist along the river, or the white breath
of headlights just before dawn burns them away.
I think of Crystal Ann in a white cotton sundress,
her shoulder drinking the afternoon sun,
and all those mad voices ranting majestically
against the latest war. I think of these
things, as the rain begins to fall in small,
measured patterns, washing the soap-streaked
lettering from the windows, the half-prints
of passing hands, bothering the dust.
It is only memory, says the rain,
and of a kind that is easily understood,
how even a few small rooms, ordinary as daylight,
become with time a sort of temple.

SHARD

Small fragments of light glinting
between the limbs of winter trees: the way

a single word
bears the spark of all others,

or how one memory
reflects another, a shard of crystal

in the window
collecting the dust the sun has cast off,

turning us back once more,
once more to the world

which grieves both our absence
and return.

MAPPING THE RAIN

I know the names of
one or two stars,
and the sun that ignites
the dust into constellations,
but tonight it is
the soft, small rain
grainy and white
in the streetlamp's
muted pulse
that directs my body
homeward,
down the black and mirrored
street, so much like
the river that I imagine
the slippery fish
swimming below,
wordless messengers
shaped like hands in prayer,
whose course is
interrupted only by
the plodding of
heavy feet.

ON TRANSLATION

What is written deep within
the heart is burned away
in ordinary light.

We mark a few words
in white ashes,
nothing more.

SOUNDS HEARD DURING AN AFTERNOON STORM IN SEPTEMBER

The wind came first, drunk and belligerent,
blowing out candles and the small stone Buddha
from the window, the electricity from these rooms
    in one exaggerated breath.
The shadows lengthen, gray and woolish,
the sound of life changes.
No televisions now.
Our music becomes the music of leaves rustling,
of rain slapping hard against window panes,
and farther down, something softer, more delicate,
    like a litter of cats
lapping from the same milk bowl.
I even hear the withered autumnal grasses,
bent down and monkish, whispering
their earth-bound mantras,
the call of a single bird, high and flinty,
like something small being opened.
Strong coffee settles in my belly.
Slender, elegant bones click as I write this now.
Even this sheet of paper, so pale and unassuming
upon the desk,
has found a way to make itself heard.

NOTES UPON THE SILENCE

Do not speak, unless it improves upon the silence.
– Buddhist saying

Sometimes the words
of a poem
arrive first, sometimes
the silence.

~~~~~

The flowers don't care
what you call them.
They know what they know,
do their best work
in silence.

~~~~~

Every silence has
a prelude,
and every prelude
an end. Spoken
or not.

~~~~~

The air casts its net;
the silence swims through
undetected.

~~~~~

Where the wind drives
these weighted summer clouds
is no concern of mine.
A fine silence lingers;
the sun returns just the same.

~~~~~

Silence is the god we pray to
when there are no words
with which to pray.

~~~~~

The language of the gods
lies in the unspoken,
the unspoken being everything but.

~~~~~

Something about silence
weighs more than the voice
it leaves behind.

~~~~~

Sometimes the memory of a voice
is all that remains — aftermath
of a long, hot rain clinging
to the body of the earth.

~~~~~

Beneath every breath
there is the thought of breath,
beneath the thought
the silence.

~~~~~

A poor student of
the Way, I have sought
perfect silence
using words
and words alone.

~~~~~

Even in the meditation hall
the silence is deceiving:
a thousand small voices fluttering
here, then there…

~~~~~

The sum of what lies
beneath the word
is not silence alone, but
the residue of all
that has been said,
and the weighted implications
of what may never be.

~~~~~

The chasm between two words
can be enormous;
the comma after love alone
keeps us wandering from
one life to the next.

~~~~~

When I was young, a woman offered me
her silence as a measure of intimacy;
but all I could discern was
the uncertain language of the rain
droning on and on…

~~~~~

Even when you speak
my name,
it's what's not said
that resonates.

~~~~~

The first time I saw you,
smiling through a slant of dusty
sunlight, I forgot every word
I had ever learned, unsure even
if the silence between us
was yours or my own.

~~~~~

Our silence was uncertain
and transitional, balanced between
moments more perfected;
but how else to learn
the language of another,
how else to know the worth
of our wordlessness,
the shadow of a promise
barely whispered, yet heard?

~~~~~

I tugged at your silence
like a thread,
until every word not spoken
came undone.

~~~~~

The small, simple words
we once let fall
with neither thought
nor hesitation
fade like the color
of a grounded leaf;
silence echoing through
the empty trees...

~~~~~

I am not sure what you are saying
with this particular silence.
I would ask, but it appears we are not speaking.
So I write these lines in your absence,
and wait for your silence to shift.

~~~~~

This silence has nothing to do
with either of us. Perhaps
someone left it here by mistake.
Send it away, love.
They may be missing it.

~~~~~

Sometimes language is
a slow-moving river,
picking up a word here,
an echo there,
a fragment of conversation
long forgotten ...

Bit by bit,
the silence on the banks
begins to recede.

~~~~~

I told her that I did not
remember saying
any of it, but that I had
certainly meant every word,
especially the silences.

~~~~~

We never could agree
on much. Even the weather
was up for debate.
In the end, she chose
her silence
and I chose mine.

~~~~~

Some voices stay with you
your entire life; others
are lost forever to the silence
between the rain.

~~~~~

It's so easy to mourn a life
that never was,
so hard to praise the long silences
that taught us to speak.

~~~~~

Any novice can play the notes
of a given instrument.
It takes a virtuoso to master
the silence.

~~~~~

One ear held
to the sound hole of
my mother's old guitar,
abandoned now
to the silence of years.

~~~~~

It's been a long time
since the autumn
brought news of you —
every leaf falling
dull side out,
every silence belonging
to someone else.

~~~~~

You, my brother, have been
silent in the earth for what seems
the length of another life.
While I go on and on about
nothing in particular ...

~~~~~

Words, of course, can never become
that which they represent.
To write the word *moon* on a page
is not to hold it as a coin in my palm;
and your name alone does not,
and will not, bring you back.
But it's not nothing.
There is a sacredness in the saying,
the simple wonder of one voice

upon the air, and the silence
so long in waiting
for this, and this alone.

~~~~~

Gone now ten years,
the sound of your laughter
grows harder
and harder to hear;
your silence a companion
familiar as the rain.

~~~~~

Some people never
truly listen.
For them, death
will be quite a shock.

~~~~~

Remember me as one
who loved silence
as much as the word;
crow tracks etched
in an empty field of snow.

~~~~~

Each time I rewrite
my epitaph, it requires fewer
and fewer words.

When only silence remains,
I know it will at last
be complete.

~~~~~

Perhaps we will recognize death
by its lack of formality,
the way it grants our silence,
so long in wandering,
a home at last.

(WRITTEN 2006-2014)

A GOOD DAY

– for Albert Huffstickler

Watching the hours
twist away in filaments
of smoke, considering
the size and shape
of the sun, the exact
length and longitude
of our longing, drinking
black coffee like
a holy sacrament,
sketching poems in
half-broken scrawl
sweated out through
daydreams in lopsided
recollection, white
shrouds of memory
approaching like
a thousand waxwings
in a cloud of dust,
knowing that time
was made to be
wasted and what
matters most is
your naked face
in warm sunlight
and letting that
sunlight love you.

THREE

Our only guide is our homesickness.

— Herman Hesse, *Steppenwolf*

MOMENT

That day outside of Berkeley, white fists
of ocean whirling below, a vast wingspan of cloud
stretched thin and ghostlike, air
thick with the salt of summer –
in that moment, weightless and electric,
you were a woman certain
you could fly, the corners of your blue eyes
drawn taut with the confidence of a crow,
the small of your chest fluttering open,
mindless and expectant – and then,
something beyond flight, beyond yearning
pulling you back, waking you human with a shudder
sharp as sunlight through sheer columns
of rain, kissing you full on the mouth
before you could know or speak its name.

THE CONSPIRACY OF NAMES

Every name is a fabrication.
You said as much the evening we met. A woman
sees a man reading at the bus stop,
or walking stoop shouldered through the rain,
and already certain conclusions are made.

Call me, you insisted, only by what you perceive.
Even if that brings forth uncertainty,
confusion, or suspicion. For my name,
like yours, was abandoned at birth.
It will take more than time for its recovery.

When we became lovers, I learned
slowly – the subtle *S* of your spine, dark calligraphy
of eyes, hair, and movement, the long
ellipses of shadow in your wake.
Touch alone became my alphabet.

When I hold you now in the nameless hours
between dark and dawn, *that* is what I call you.
When I speak your name, it is with
the common understanding of conspirators,
whose stories must correspond perfectly –

if they are to be believed at all.

LINES

I like how the lines of your eyes
fan outward when you smile,
even while sleeping;
roads that go only so far
then descend into thought, memory,
residual laughter.

I think of the immense longing
to travel those roads,
the snakelike bend of a country lane,
subtle persistence
of a wagon trail slicing through prairie,
grass grown long as horsewhips,
though the trail is still
discernible
a century after all have left.

TRAINS

There are times when I see us as passengers
on separate trains, passing each other
at those ghost – early hours of night,
small shards of light signaling
between the cars; the other riders,
if there are any, dead asleep
in the distances they have created.

I see our reflections merge
in the windows, mouth to mouth,
passing through one another –
the outline of a tree where my eye had been,
the moon blazing through your temple,
white and feverish – the image cast,
for a moment of eternity, across
a field of stubble in some Midwestern town
that might even have been home
had we stopped long enough
to recognize it.

MEMO

Found your name and number slipped
seamlessly between *The Waning of the Middles Ages*
and Rexroth's *Sacramental Acts* – a relic
rediscovered after years in hiding,
the small, thin paper yellowed
as a nicotine stain with age,
the heart-shaped stencil ragged round
the edges and fading. I cannot now bring you forth
from this lifetime of otherness.
Your face becomes the face of distance,
a landscape concealed
behind layers of years and neglect;
your laughter indiscernible.
I speak your name
out loud, its music both foreign and familiar,
the way any prayer or blasphemy
endlessly repeated becomes
neither, only the truth of the sound itself.
It is in this place we may yet meet, speaking openly
of all we failed to cultivate
in the bright memory of the unknown
that was meant for us all along.

NOW

I told you once when we were young that
we would someday meet again.
Now, the years flown past, the letters
unwritten, I am not so certain.

It is autumn. There are toothaches hidden
in this wind, there are those determined
to bring forth winter at any cost.
I am resigned to dark blonde shadows

at stoplights, lost in the roadmaps of leaves
which point in every direction at once.
But I am wearing the shirt you stitched
two separate lifetimes ago. It is old

and falling to ash, yet every button blooms
the flowers of your design. I think of this
and I am happy, to have kissed
your mouth with the force of language,

to have spoken your name at all.

MORNING POEM

The halved orange on the butcher's block,
pulsing imperceptibly,
warming dust of sunlight seeping in,
pale radiance of your thigh by which I read;
your hair upon the pillow a marriage
of mandarin and blood,
where the fabric folds and distant crows
cast their shadows on your sleeping temples.
I leave this poem upon the table
where the wine glasses have been left
and the slender knife from the night before
has been quietly removed.

FOR MY BROTHER
ON HIS FORTY-FIRST BIRTHDAY

In December things start getting serious.
You know what I mean. The trees
grow lean and solemn, and only the hardened criminals
of the bird world remain. A paper bag
billowing down the frozen road
makes a noise like distant thunder.
Cats are scarce. Love is stored in secret places.
Rivers run beneath the level of thought,
going nowhere and back again.
In December we scatter rose petals
in honor of your birthday, red petals blown
into the loose configuration of
a heart upon the newly-white earth
that is your grave. We take long steps back
to the car, hands bitten by wind,
our silence precise.
Every distance here is great:
the leaving, the stillness, the slow and
knowing return.

MIDWAY MOTEL

You might find yourself here unexpectedly, with neither direction nor intent. Say you are just passing through, no fixed address, and the less you say about where you're from the more at ease others seem to be. Say your wife found the letter you had intended for the eyes of another, or that other received the words intended for no one. Now you lie in the in-between, locked out of that other part of yourself. Down the hall you can hear coughing, muffled conversations from TV screens, the clack-clacking of typewriter keys like tiny gunshots echoing. You lie in a bed worn down by others, the desire of others, green-gray light from the freeway below framing the edges of windows and doors. Sipping lukewarm beer at three in the morning, you wonder where it all went; and who or what it might be heading toward now.

TORNADO

Just beyond the hem of the lake's blue skirt
the sky turned suddenly jaundiced,

a weighted stillness, not quite your own,
descended, and even the black pine

and birch hovered motionless
in a calm that bore no calmness at all.

And for what must have been the briefest
of moments you gazed, a child of seven,

transfixed on the sinewy black thread
of the storm, its form swaying,

tearing the fabric of the horizon,
throwing bits of cloud and gravel dust

as dogs and kids scurried into the small, white cabins
which suddenly looked as though they were

made to be thrown all along, something
stolen from the set of someone else's epic.

And years later you would not remember
how it was you were pulled indoors,

or whose arm it was that lifted you
with the force of a blow bringing you to safety,

nor how the storm at once lifted, *lifted*,
like a needle from a phonograph

above the roofs of trees still trembling;
and when you looked out again

it was through brown sheets of mud
slapped across the windows

the dark fragrance of earthworms
seeping through the slats,

beyond which the world shone as green
and peaceful as it ever would again.

ON THE DEATH OF A GIRAFFE
AT COMO ZOO

The neck went first, as if suddenly
realizing both the brilliance
and absurdity of its design – pulled first
from side to side in drunken sway;
then down, down, by skull and by chance,
the small bricks of vertebrae
collapsing, matchstick legs brave
but unsteady, confused
as the children were confused,
but no one – neither the parents
with faces blank as bars of soap, nor
the zookeepers rushing in
with their sad, clumsy hands
waving – could explain
this dark, impromptu ballet:
immense onyx eyes with brushstroke lashes
more beautiful than the lashes
of any woman, turning
upward toward the empty sky
and all that good blonde sunlight spilling
out onto the ground at once.

WASHING HER HAIR

It's the way he sometimes
approaches, casual as a shrug
or a tune hummed softly
in the milk–syrup light
of early morning, his hips
meeting hers at that good, soft
country of lower back
as she stands
in wordless obeisance
at the kitchen sink
eyes still puffy with sleep,
wetting her hair
in mild distraction
to face a day of ordinariness
and distraction more
agitated and pressing;
and taking a small dollop
of shampoo, he begins
to lather, to gently lather
her wet tangles of hair,
small bells of water
on shoulder and neck
drinking the light
one by one, as she smiles
knowingly, and in this
way, without words
or formality, the day begins.

CROWDS

When exactly did all women become one
and one woman become all? It is
as if each body were threaded together
by strands of invisible light,
the way crowds sometimes blur
in the shimmering heat of late summer —
each memory a shard that reflects the other.
I love you now with the love
of thousands, and speak your name
even in the names of others.

I KNOW

I know the world we perceive is only
the world we perceive; and yet
at this moment, my flesh inside your flesh,
your legs wrapped tight around me,
your mouth encircling mine
with the unyielding force
of eternity, even the self is swallowed
and forgotten. I am a man
in love with my illusions.

THE LEAVING

I will not miss this place but for
the paraffin glow of the young nurse's face,
blonde and almond-eyed,
strange comfort of the flashlight's
blinking on and off as she makes her
nightly rounds, seemingly without steps,
to check if you are still breathing,
kneeling at the bedside to ask,
Are you still awake? Do you need a pill?
as outside the window a dull gray
snow is falling into absence,
and you cradle a thought no longer there,
as if it mattered, as if anything
but her cool, soft hands offering
the drowse-inducing Eucharist
made sense anymore; as if a mind
drawing circles to mark eternity
and Xs for all the suffering
that implies could contain anything more
than the purposeful spark of fine,
subtle hips turning toward the door,
a leaving so gentle and assured
that it makes you feel nearly at home
in this world once again.

MY BROTHER'S TATTOO

He might have chosen the Sacred Heart,
symbol of compassion both eternal
and all-consuming. The idea of redemption
like a bruise upon the shoulder.

Might have chosen a former lover's name;
or, more provocatively, the naked form of a woman,
representation of flesh carved into flesh,
the body that will not be denied. He chose

instead to be engraved upon his right forearm,
the too-familiar image of the grim reaper —
the scythe, the hourglass, the bony grimace
emerging through a cloak full of night,

its shadow longer than any story invented.
He must have known, I think, he would
not be here long, must have carried what we
all carry a bit closer beneath the skin.

And this is the image he departs with —
reminder of the commonality
we endlessly attempt to evade, the face beneath
the face; an image that lasts only as long

as the flesh to which it clings.

PARTING GESTURES

1.

I'll come back in a thousand years
when you will have perhaps
forgiven me. In the meantime,
this brittle, rice paper heart
works quite well for shorter poems.

2.

The clouds today are the color
of winter. More wind than water,
these clouds have no form
but formlessness, six long fingers
reaching back into the night.

3.

November. The wind brings forth
memory deep in the bones.
The thirst for dry leaves
is both ancient and familiar,
the moon trembling with water.

4.

The night goes back so far
yet cannot find daylight again.
The heart that set out
so long ago in search of itself
has returned alone.

5.

The lines in your hand
reach back farther than you
could ever imagine. Most of that
journey you have forgotten.
Yet my hand in yours remembers.

6.

The hand we perceive as waving
knows neither hello nor goodbye,
nor the difference between
departure and a woman sweeping
the hair from her eyes.

FOUR
New Poems

I must remember never to say I remember.
— Ray Davies

SKIPPING A STONE ALONG SUPERIOR

You find a stone that has taken its time — more than a thousand years, in fact, to uncover its truest form. You feel its unassuming weight, rub it gently between thumb and forefinger, as if trying to decipher a message. But, of course, it speaks only stone, and you have long forgotten the few words and phrases you once knew. With a snap of the wrist you send it scudding across the surface of the water — four times, five times, six — before it disappears into the undifferentiated blue. It is doubtful you will ever return to this spot, or that you could find your way here again. But if you do, you know this stone will be here, unseen, shifting imperceptibly, making its long way back to shore.

IN THE WINGS

For a moment, none of this makes
sense – the crowded voices murmuring
from the stage, muffled yet familiar,
the heat-pulse of angled lights…

Someone rushes by with a large wooden
box, a half-wilted fern with roots
reaching blindly into air.
Things change here so quickly.

Only the smells linger for longer
than a song: warm comfort of stately wood,
velvet and dust mingled with sweat,
of your own skin breathing wool.

For a moment, everything slows to a waltz.
Your swallow echoes. You await
the gesture, somehow remembered,
that is your cue for entrance.

You trust the words will come.

REREADING THE OLD CHINESE POETS

Always there is a scene of
departure, an old friend or love

setting out at dusk
toward a world unknowable,

always the longing
for stillness and sameness

in a life that flows
in one unyielding direction,

the odd comfort of absence
and the hope of return –

in the blazing of autumn leaves,
the gray, stoic mountains

clouded by mist and memory,
the wine of the moon

beginning to tremble
in a glass already drained dry.

DISAPPEARING IN SAN FRANCISCO

It happened only once: wandering the slick,
uneven streets along Telegraph Hill,
when the fog bounded up from the ocean,
from the earth, from every possible
angle, like the breath of an adolescent god,
petulant, determined only in confusion.
And for one moment, brief as a shudder, all
the eye could hold was swallowed,
and you stood suddenly outside the body,
an orphan of the flesh, beyond the reference
points of streets, buildings, trees, beyond
the humming persistence of the tangible.
But of course the wind threw out a few
frayed lines, enough to glance a patch of pavement,
the rustling green of shrouded leaves,
and the shapely leg of the young woman
walking beside you. You came back,
and the moment was abandoned
like a shell along the beach echoing,
left like so many distances between two
united long ago, as you began the steep slopes
downward, the astonishingly bright hues
of houses rushing up to meet you.

ODE TO MY SMITH-CORONA SD-650

I have not forgotten you,
dearest machine,
you who made me believe I might
somehow be a writer –
long before the slightest
evidence, long before
a single sigh or sentence emerged
unscathed.

You, an extravagant expense
for someone so young,
wrapped as I was in that gray, unassuming
poverty. I have not forgotten –
how could I? – the small, clipped thunder
of each letter echoing, so insistent
in the silence of those smallest hours,
the fabric of the page indented
with the force of your
endless imagining.

Was it you who was driving all along?
It hardly mattered. I was happy
to follow your every turn,
the page a beginner's map continually thrown
to the wind behind us.

Now you lie silent and noble upon the shelf.
Now the last factory has closed.
No more of your kind emerging
for young hands and minds to master.
But I remember; I remember
keeping the neighbors awake with the electric
pulse of your engine,

feeling that new and singular freedom,
playing your smooth, fine keys
when there was no music in all the world
to be found but our own.

AT THE SPARKLE LAUNDROMAT
ON RICE STREET

The teenagers are bored, having nowhere else to go, not
wanting to go home to the drab familiarity of housing projects
and apartment complexes. We too are directionless, but
directionless in the same place and time – between jobs,
between loves, between ambitions; we are loitering without
intent. Hank Williams echoes from a small dusty speaker,
quarters tumble from the change machine, pool balls click with
soft indifference. The ceiling-high windows are veiled with
steam, impossible to tell at first glance if it is summer or winter,
daylight or evening. There is no stampede of years here, no
memory rushing in either direction, insistent on its own
inherent beauty – only the rhythm of machines in cycle, that
constant turning without arrival. We could come back decades
from now, pick up where we left off, wait it out for one more
song before returning to the world again.

MY BROTHER RETURNS

My brother returns from time to time
to rewrite the details of his death

upon my dreams. And sometimes
the dream appears the more real.

I can't say just why. Perhaps the dead
suspect we have grown

complacent with the facts – or worse,
that we have somehow mistaken

facts for the truth. Perhaps
they too have grown weary with

the same demise year upon year,
and have altered the landscape

of our grief, if only for a moment.
I have lived here long enough

to know that every day of waking
is likewise a day of mourning;

yet every mourning can be assuaged
by a single touch, or a word

spoken through the trembling dark.

IT DEPENDS ON WHICH WAY
YOU FACE THE LIGHT

Snow. Snow. The only word spoken today.
One insistent hush upon the other.
Everything becomes a kind of secret now,
every walk becomes a long one.
The sky drains to the color of drywall;
the small moons of children's faces gaze
out from schoolroom windows.
Thumbprints of white whirl across the glass.
From below, the sound of someone shoveling,
like pages of a book being turned.
And the birds – the birds, wherever
they are – tell you nothing.
And they do so again and again.

LANDSCAPE

Calm simplicity of the hardwood
floor, measured by miles
and miles of thought – one page of sunlight
open where you left it, unable
or unwilling to read further.
The voices have all passed through,
the sighs of love slipped beneath
other doors without warning.
What to say now of the claw-footed bathtub
glowing cool and spotless
as a snowdrift, soft cotton plains
of the bed not slept in?
The silence of these rooms
bears no malevolence, not the absence
you presume, but welcomes
your return like a mother, like a lover
faithful as time. Shadows thread
the familiar to the familiar; the landscape
on the wall goes on and on.

THE SAME SUN, THE SAME MOON

Tonight the rain is talking too fast to be understood.
I write in haste, but make no sense of it at all.

Gray starlings congregate beneath the crumbling eaves;
their voices are small, but each a part of the all.

I missed those early lectures on renouncing the earth.
Without the dust that brought me here, I am nothing at all.

Some days the photographs on the wall simply run dry,
our shadows too longing to walk away from it all.

Even now you come and go, absent-minded as the wind,
your love hiding between the nothing and the all.

Naturally, I wanted to be duped by such love;
I became a gambler who wishes only to lose it all.

Still, we see the same sun and moon passing daily;
which is to say, we hardly see them at all.

PLAINSONG

The days move so quickly now. What are they running from?
Even our shadows race past us, never to be seen again.

What to do with a Northern winter but create new myths?
The snowflakes vary, but the sky repeats itself again and again.

In such flat country, we long for the roundness of earth.
We lie close at night, our bodies rising again and again.

We forget so easily that even these bodies are on loan;
whatever we may accumulate, there will be no loss, no gain.

A man could walk for miles here and never disappear.
One self continues walking, another comes back again.

I have made so many bad turns and returned only to seeking.
Breaking the rules, I learn only which to break again.

Perhaps all wonder lies in the most ordinary life.
If we wait a thousand eons, this moment will not come again.

IF I WERE TO CHOOSE BUT ONE

If I were to choose but one moment
for you to remember
of that long-ago autumn,
I would remind you of how the moon
shot above the narrow trees
that night while driving home,
blazing and sudden as another world, so large
the sky could not contain it; how
we pulled the car to the side of the road
laughing in wonder, because beauty
so often is equally absurd.
I would remind you only of this
moment, of that childlike astonishment
between two who refused
to know better - and how it all
disappeared as we rounded the next corner.
Yet even you, my only witness
through these dim corridors of years,
might find it hard to remember – might
find it hard to believe at all.

WHEN AT LAST OUR BODIES MET

When at last our bodies met,
after years of circling
like boxers in the ring,
our words departed
as birds startled into flight,

and all we had spoken
and meant to forget
in two separate lifetimes
became one breath
then another,

scattered like safety nets
upon the open air.

LISTENING FOR BIRDS, EARLY SPRING

From the bed she can hear
them, chattering softly
outside the curtained window –
those nameless, invisible birds,
ghost birds come to call
just beyond the realm
of winter's drab undoing.
And what do I hear?
My breathing, then hers besides me,
soft whir of the ceiling fan,
dull metronome of bedside clock;
then, back to her breathing,
the unhurried rhythm of
ocean thousands of miles removed.
But outside there is singing,
half notes and whole
clustered upon the open spring air.
I want to lie here
a few moments longer,
listening and nothing more.
I want the music to find me,
contentedly unaware, want simply
to hear what she hears.

EACH DAY THE SUN MAKES US

Each day the sun makes us believe
it will last forever, and then
disappears again into the earth,
the last of its light thin as the thread
of ink that signs your name
in haste or desperation, one dark letter
indecipherable from the next.

EVEN YOU

When I first saw you, I'd already been inventing you for years. Who knows what shadow you conjured while considering me. I could have been anybody. Or no one at all. Years later, I no longer believe in the unyielding line of Fate, but am ill-equipped to decipher the hand of Chance. Perhaps there is somewhere between, a somewhere not quite, where we can meet again for the first time. Call it that time of day where the day breaks apart, moves elsewhere. And that elsewhere begins to seep in. This is the darkness your eyes are accustomed to – those two separate infinities where words fail, as they so often do. I close the book and the words go on, drinking up the dark, unable to explain their noble intentions. Unable to describe even you.

HOT

My God, it was hot –
unbearably so – the first night
together in that cramped
attic apartment,
trying and failing to sleep,
twisting and sighing
between heavy cotton sheets,
a wave of heat-damp breath
unable to reach its shore.

Twice you stumbled out of bed
to fill your tumbler with ice, twice
to stand beneath the cool
stream of the shower's neck.
But the heat droned on,
giving way only to more heat
until even the moon seemed hot,
a white stone burning
through the gauze of the window.

And when we thought
morning might never arrive,
it did, shrugging and unembroidered;
and we moved slowly,
drugged by the groggy air,
hardly noticing the damp shroud
of our bodies imprinted
in the bed, fading like stars
into the blue expanse of day.

AFTER

There's a part of me I left behind, lingering
like smoke between two younger versions of ourselves.
I am not sure of the exact moment.
Perhaps it was when you stole away
from the bed to the bathroom in that gray-lavender
nightgown and the moon met the soft curve
of your leg just so. I do not know.
But I left it there without regret,
like any good pupil would.
And when we parted, we parted for all time.
This much we know, or think we do.
But when Chia Tao came down
from the mountain – after years of sitting
like the mountain itself – he didn't
come back all the way.

YOUR SILENCE, AGAIN

Once, I tried calling you
from a rusted blue phone booth
outside the old Super-Valu
beneath a cold sheen of night sky;
I was ten, and dreaming again,
your number suddenly
familiar as the bones in my hand.
But the gray stars pierced,
and the bloodless mumble that
answered was my own,
startling me back at once
to this long, intractable silence
I still refused to believe
or call my own.

MARKINGS

Markings along the highway,
like bruises beneath the skin, fade
with the passing of days,
the simple persistence of rain writing its name
continuously upon our own.
The birds grow lean as the branches,
new shadows bleed into the old.
The evidence is cleared away,
the summer blacktop smoothed
and stretched like fresh canvas, where
one boot heel was dragged,
sparking like flint across the road,
and handprints on the hood of the car
fluttered like dusty wings against
the dark and mirrored sky.

THIS LIFE IS SO STUBBORN

In your hospital bed you seemed so heavy, as if swallowing the earth through endless tangles of wire. Perhaps we take on the weight of every existence we turn away from. Or perhaps it is memory that drags us under in the end. But this life is so stubborn. It refuses to be ours, yet refuses to be anything other. When I think of you now, brother, it is with the failure to grasp even the simplest leaf, stone, or passing cloud. It is the failure I hold most dear.

RESERVOIR

Over the years I have trained
myself to think of you
less and less. Not because
your memory brings with it regret
both sharp and direct,
but because each time I return
to the reservoir – sacred to me as
the sunrise – something
small but substantial
is subtracted.

I visit less often, out of caution
and my need for keeping
things whole – so afraid am I
of further loss, so afraid
you will disappear
completely.

UNFATHOMABLE

Today I write just enough
that the words,
one by one
or in small constellations,
disappear into
the ink-blue trees of evening,
and all that remains
is that feeling –
the unfathomable hush
of the world
unnamed
and unspoken for.

photo: Jordana Torgeson

Greg Watson's work has appeared in numerous literary journals, including *The Seattle Review*, *Tulane Review*, and *Poetry East*. His most recent collections are *What Music Remains, Things You Will Never See Again,* and *The Distance Between Two Hands*. He lives in Saint Paul, Minnesota.